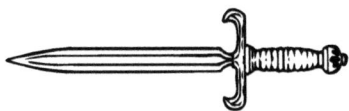

WORLDVIEW GUIDE

MACBETH

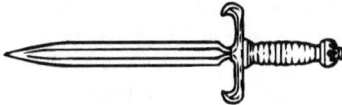

Brian Kohl

canonpress
Moscow, Idaho

Published by Canon Press
P.O. Box 8729, Moscow, Idaho 83843
800.488.2034 | www.canonpress.com

Brian Kohl, *Worldview Guide for Macbeth*, 1st Ed. Revised
Copyright ©2019 by Brian Kohl.
Cited page numbers come from the Canon Classics edition of the play (2016),
www.canonpress.com/books/canon-classics.

Cover design by James Engerbretson
Cover illustration by Forrest Dickison
Interior design by Valerie Anne Bost and James Engerbretson

Printed in the United States of America.

A free end-of-book test and answer key are available for download at
www.canonpress.com/ClassicsQuizzes

Library of Congress Cataloging-in-Publication Data
Kohl, Brian, author.
The tragedy of Macbeth / Brian Kohl.
Other titles: Worldview guide
Canon Classics second edition. | Moscow, ID : Canon Press,
   [2019] | Series: Canon classics worldview series
LCCN 2018053179 | ISBN 9781944503062 (paperback : alk. paper)
LCSH: Shakespeare, William, 1564-1616. Macbeth—Juvenile
   literature.
Classification: LCC PR2823 .K64 2019 | DDC 822.3/3--dc23
LC record available at https://lccn.loc.gov/2018053179

19 20 21 22 23 24   9 8 7 6 5 4 3

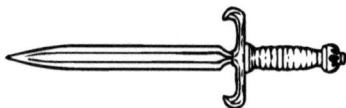

CONTENTS

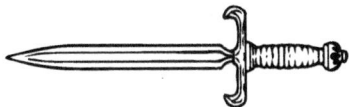

INTRODUCTION

Perhaps the most vivid testament to the power of *Macbeth* is that actors consider the play itself bad luck. At least, none of the cast are supposed to mention it by name backstage: instead it's to be called "the Scottish play." And the themes seem to justify this reaction: *Macbeth* is an unhappy and bloody story in which ambition proves to be the harshest master and men's lives little more than the playthings of witches.

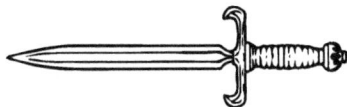

THE WORLD AROUND

Although *Macbeth* was actually completed in 1606, three years *after* Queen Elizabeth I's death,[1] the play is viewed as another product of the Elizabethan Golden Age. This period of history is stuffed with a host of culture-changers, including Edmund Spenser, Shakespeare himself, Sir Francis Bacon, Sir Walter Raleigh, Sir Francis Drake and many other sirs.

But for the English, the dawn of this new century wasn't necessarily a time of optimism. Instead, it was the *end* of an era: Elizabeth left no heir, and the passing of the last of the Tudors—a line of monarchs that had ruled England for the past 120 years—must have been unsettling. All in all, the transfer of power went smoothly: King James VI of Scotland became King James I in 1603,

---

1. Circa 1606 is the date according to most scholars. The source for much of my information about Shakespeare's life is A.D. Cousins, ed., *The Shakespeare Encyclopedia* (Buffalo, NY: Firefly Books, 2009), s.v. "Macbeth."

joining England and Scotland under one ruler at long last. And there were only two serious efforts to get rid of the new king: one by kidnapping (which contributed to Sir Walter Raleigh's eventual execution much later), and one by explosion (the notorious Gunpowder Plot of November 5th). Both attempts were thwarted. So, compared to the previous struggles associated with succession (e.g., the Wars of the Roses), it *was* a smooth transition.

But in 1606 the rest of the world wasn't sitting around waiting for Shakespeare's darkest tragedy. In Spain, Cervantes had just finished *Don Quixote*. In North America, all the European powers were hurrying to get a stake in the New World. Within three years of *Macbeth*'s completion, the English would have Jamestown in Virginia (which is named after Elizabeth, "the Virgin Queen"), the Dutch would have the first European post on Manhattan Island, and the Spanish would have founded Santa Fe.

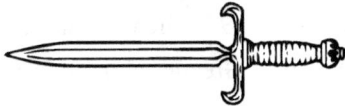

ABOUT THE AUTHOR

Much of William Shakespeare's life story must be deduced from other accounts of the period, because Shakespeare left little written record—at least, little beyond his vast contribution to English literature.[2] He was born in Stratford-upon-Avon, a country town in the middle of England, in 1564—the same year Michelangelo and John Calvin both died.

As a child, he lived through an outbreak of the Black Death and was "classically educated" at the local grammar school. At eighteen years old, Shakespeare married Anne Hathaway, who was eight years older than he and already

---

2. A few pariahs have argued that Shakespeare himself was not the author of the plays. Many of these theories are obviously crazy, but the conspiracy theorists among you might enjoy them nonetheless. For example, Joseph Sobran and others reason that Edward de Vere, 17th Earl of Oxford, fits as the author of plays and sonnets much better than a modestly educated country actor. See Sobran, *Alias Shakespeare* (New York: Free Press, 1997).

pregnant with their first child. After this, he apparently began work as an actor in London. No evidence exists of his playwriting until 1592, when he was blasted by a competitor named Robert Greene, who called Shakespeare "an upstart Crow…[who] supposes he is able to bombast out a blank verse as the best of you…"[3] It's around this time that scholars have dated his first plays—*Henry VI, Richard III,* and *Comedy of Errors.* He became quite wealthy, even purchasing some ownership in the Globe Theater. Based on his plays, Shakespeare was a true Renaissance man of life experience, somehow familiar with the noblest courts in Europe and the bawdiest taverns.

Some scandal has attended his work. The Victorians were perturbed enough by his recurrent vulgarity to bowdlerize his plays, and whether his sonnets—many addressed to another man—are homosexual in intent is a debated topic. (Just for the record, C.S. Lewis argued the love in the sonnets isn't erotic.[4]) Rumors of other extramarital affairs have persisted, and it doesn't help that in his will, all he left Anne (after thirty-some years together) was his "second best bed."[5]

---

3. This quote and other facts about Shakespeare's life also from A.D. Cousins, ed., *The Shakespeare Encyclopedia* (Buffalo, NY: Firefly Books, 2009).

4. C.S. Lewis, *English Literature in the Sixteenth Century Excluding Drama* (Oxford: Oxford, 1973), 503.

5. Of course, as with most things Shakespearean, we don't actually even know the true (in)significance of a "second best bed."

Regardless, Shakespeare died in 1616 with his reputation forever cemented as "the Bard of Avon"—wordsmith of the stories that have been a driving force behind half a millennium of human imagination.

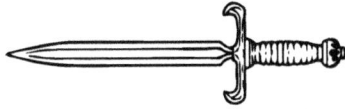

WHAT OTHER
NOTABLES SAID

The existence of the word *bardolatry*—excessive adoration of all things Shakespearian—should speak volumes about Shakespeare's status. The critic William Hazlitt found it hard to identify Shakespeare's best trait: "The characteristic of Chaucer is intensity; of Spenser, remoteness; of Milton, elevation; of Shakespeare, every thing."[6] And Romantic poet Samuel Taylor Coleridge—perhaps the quintessential bardolator—waxed eloquent about his universality as well: "Our myriad-minded Shakespeare...becomes all things, yet forever remaining himself."[7]

Everyone knows and loves Shakespeare—even if it's more that they would love to *have* read him, rather than

---

6. William Hazlitt, "On Shakespeare and Milton" (1818), English Poetry 1579-1830, http://spenserians.cath.vt.edu/TextRecord.php?-textsid=36138 (accessed 4/1/2016).

7. Samuel Taylor Coleridge, *Biographia Literaria* Vol. 2, Ch. 15 (1817).

actually to do it. But this shouldn't take away from our appreciation. Robert Graves put it this way: "The remarkable thing about Shakespeare is that he is really very good—in spite of all the people who say he is very good."[8]

So, it might surprise you that some famous authors really didn't care for him. Neither Voltaire nor Tolstoy were fans, but perhaps the most dramatic of all was George Bernard Shaw, who wrote of Shakespeare, "The intensity of my impatience with him occasionally reaches such a pitch, that it would positively be a relief to me to dig him up and throw stones at him."[9]

There *was* one author worse than Shakespeare in Shaw's exalted opinion… Homer. Good company, I suppose.

---

8. Robert Graves, "Sayings of the Week," *The Observer,* Dec. 6, 1964.
9. George Bernard Shaw, *Shaw on Shakespeare*, ed. by Edwin Wilson (New York: Arno, 1980), 56.

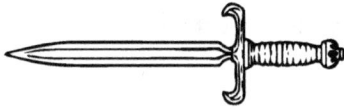

PLOT SUMMARY, SETTING, AND CHARACTERS

- *Setting: Scotland in the 11th century*
- *Duncan:* the aging King of Scotland[10]
- *Malcolm:* King Duncan's son and heir (Prince of Cumberland)
- *Donalbain:* King Duncan's second son
- *Thane of Cawdor:* a traitorous nobleman whose title is soon given to Macbeth
- *Macdonwald:* another traitorous nobleman
- *Macbeth:* an ambitious Scottish nobleman (the Thane of Glamis) and the title character

---

10. Most of Macbeth's main characters and the witches' prophecies were inspired by (or taken from) Holinshed's *Chronicles of England, Scotland, and Ireland*, a popular account of England, Scotland, and Ireland published during Shakespeare's lifetime. Shakespeare "improved" the story all over the place, so it's not necessary to read the historical context.

- *Lady Macbeth:* Macbeth's wife who is more ruthless than her husband
- *Macduff:* a loyal Scottish nobleman (the Thane of Fife)
- *Banquo:* another Scottish nobleman and Macbeth's closest friend
- *Fleance:* Banquo's son
- *Three Witches:* Three servants of Hecate, Queen of Witches, who prophesy to Macbeth; also called the Weird ("Fate") Sisters

Macbeth begins and ends with the death of traitors, and treachery and revenge drive its plot. Macbeth—a thane (chieftain and general) of the Scottish king, Duncan—has just vividly ended the life of the traitor Macdonwald by "unseam[ing] him from the nave to the chaps" (p. 2).[11]

After the traitor's head has been stuck up on his castle walls, Macbeth rides back to the king with his fellow general Banquo and they bump into gruesome figures on the moor. The Three Witches are waiting for Macbeth and prophesy to him and Banquo: Macbeth is already the Thane of Glamis, but he will be Thane of Cawdor—and eventually King of Scotland. The prophecy is vague besides those two specifics (and it only gets vaguer after the witches

---

11. Page numbers throughout come from the Canon Classics edition of *Macbeth* (Moscow, ID: Canon Press, 2016). There are, sadly, no standard line numbers for Shakespeare's works.

tell Banquo that Banquo's descendants will be king, though he won't), but Macbeth only cares about the "promotions."

In feudal Scotland, a thane was a chieftain with holdings from the king, so all treachery was biting the hand that fed you, in a very personal way. And Macbeth finds that King Duncan is so pleased with Macbeth's killing of Macdonwald that he immediately makes him Thane of Cawdor—for the previous thane had just been sentenced to death for colluding with the Norwegians. Macbeth can think of little besides the specifics of the prophecy—*Glamis then Cawdor then Scotland*—and rides like the wind to let Lady Macbeth know two of three prophecies have come true...and that King Duncan wanted to stay that night at Macbeth's castle on Dunsinane Hill.

Unfortunately, Lady Macbeth is the most virulently ambitious creature you can imagine, and her sole desire is now to get her husband to murder old King Duncan, drug and frame his chamberlains, and fulfill the final part of the prophecy. Convincing him is surprisingly easy, and by the next morning, Duncan and the chamberlains are dead, the heirs have fled to England under suspicion, and Macbeth and his lady are king and queen. All is right with the world!

Well, not really. "Blood will have blood" (p. 51), and Macbeth is drawn deeper into a cycle of bloodshed and guilt. He kills his friend Banquo to prevent that part of the witches' prophecy, and then is driven mad by Banquo's ghost. He goes back to the witches, and gets three more prophecies: first, that he should "beware Macduff", that "none of woman born" can kill him, and that he'll be victorious until Birnam Wood comes against him (pp. 59-60).

Macduff has fled to join Malcolm, but Macbeth murders his wife and son anyways. Lady Macbeth feels the guilt of all this blood, and she loses her sanity even as Macbeth grows more and more paranoid. Malcolm and Macduff enlist the help of the English, and the combined army arrives at Dunsinane, fulfilling the witches' prophecies.

The play ends with a second traitor beheaded, except this time, of course, that traitor is Macbeth.

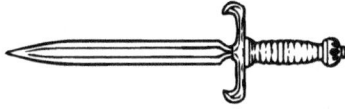

WORLDVIEW ANALYSIS

Perhaps the most famous line in this play comes after Macbeth is told of his wife's suicide: "Life," he says to himself, "...is a tale / Told by an idiot, full of sound and fury, / Signifying nothing" (p. 86). Of course, if Macbeth means there's no rhyme or reason to his own story, he's wrong; he knows that and so do we.

Any attempt to make sense of the sound and the fury should start with Macbeth's own character. We know more about Macbeth than anyone else—he speaks close to seven hundred lines in the play. (In comparison, the second-most lines go to Lady Macbeth—and she has only about two hundred fifty.) So an important scene where Macbeth *forgets* to talk should stand out to us. But that's what seems to happen when the generals first encounter the witches (pp. 6-7). Macbeth is twice described as "rapt," and Banquo is the one who cross-examines the witches. Macbeth doesn't speak at length until they start to vanish. Afterwards, Banquo (and the readers) wonder if the witches have some ulterior motive. Macbeth starts daydreaming about an "imperial theme" (p. 9). We'd be slightly suspicious if we happened upon three weird sisters on a blighted heath, so what is it that seems to hold Macbeth spellbound?

Macbeth gives us the answer: "I have no spur / To prick the sides of my intent, but only / Vaulting ambition, which o'erleaps itself, / And falls on the other." Macbeth is hungry for power. Even after Duncan makes him Thane of Cawdor as well as Glamis—better than any other of the noblemen—Macbeth's ambition won't let him enjoy it—because Malcolm has been named Prince of Cumberland, heir to the throne, and that this is one more "step" he must fall on or vault over.

Of course, Macbeth's underlying premise—*more for you means less for me*—is a basic human sin, familiar even to toddlers: it's called selfishness. It's true that there can't be two kings. But the second premise—*I cannot be happy unless I am king*—is flawed. And Macbeth's conclusion—*therefore I should kill to be happy*—is evil as well as selfish. In that sense, *Macbeth* is a terrifying look at the divine promise that "whoever exalts himself will be humbled" (Lk. 14:11). Once Macbeth prayed, "Stars, hide your fires! / Let not light see my black and deep desires," he put the wheels in motion, and there was no way to stop them from eventually crushing him—at least, no way to stop *and still be king*. Ambition is a harsh master.

But the power of the play is that Macbeth's decisions seem reasonable—or at least understandable—until he actually stabs Duncan...and even after that, maybe up to the point where he has Banquo murdered! (After and including that betrayal, Macbeth acts "brainsickly" by any standard, to use this play's wonderful adverb.) Shakespeare masterfully creates the illusion that assassinating your king *might* be an acceptable option, right up until it happens, and the reader realizes it isn't acceptable. That's what makes this play's atmosphere *feel* so terrifying.

So, how does Shakespeare make us sympathetic to Macbeth? Two ways.

First, he makes Macbeth an admirable character. Before the general turns assassin, his ambition and military prowess are important for a thane to have, and he is good at using force. His king is more pleased with him than any other thane (two holdings, Glamis and Cawdor, remember). There's something impressive about the "at least I'll die with harness on my back" approach to life. Everyone sees that: Once Duncan is killed and the blame pinned on his disappeared sons, Macbeth is the obvious choice for king. In this case, as James P. Hammersmith puts it, Macbeth has less of a "tragic flaw" than a "predisposition" that happens to work out tragically due to its surroundings.[12]

---

12. James P. Hammersmith, "Shakespeare and the Tragic Virtue," *Southern Humanities Review* 24.3 (Summer 1990), 245-54, http://www.jsu.edu/depart/english/gates/shtragcv.htm (accessed Apr. 7, 2016). Hammersmith argues that Aristotle had very little impact in

Hammersmith goes so far as to call Macbeth's political and martial ability his "tragic virtue." Shakespeare leaves us wondering, perhaps if circumstances had been different and Duncan hadn't stayed the night...perhaps if Lady Macbeth hadn't been quite so ferocious, or the chamberlains quite so easy to bamboozle...might Macbeth have continued his rise to prominence in Scottish politics without daring to murder for the throne?

But of course, when it mattered, Macbeth's ambition *did* stumble him. As has been observed, sometimes our so-called virtues are what we need to repent of most.

The second reason we empathize with Macbeth's plight has to do with the play's genre. Elizabethan revenge tragedy contains the common themes of murder, madness, revenge, and supernatural intervention.[13] We've already touched on murder. Madness comes at the end. But it's the supernatural element that most draw us to pity Macbeth the man. It's the witches.

Macbeth's ambition helps him get over his natural aversion to witches as soon as the first prophecy comes true:

Elizabethan England, and attempting to apply Aristotle's tragic categories to Shakespeare's plays in a wooden way is somewhat anachronistic. In fact, he says, a tragic virtue is more compelling than a tragic flaw. Of course, the distinction between a "trait" or "predisposition" that causes your downfall and a "flaw" that causes your downfall seems a bit pedantic.

13. In his introductory note to *Hamlet*, Shane Weller identifies these four things as "stock elements," although there are more common themes than just these in Elizabethan tragedies. *Four Great Tragedies* (Mineola, NY: Dover, 1992).

"Two truths are told, / As happy prologues to the swelling act / Of the imperial theme… / This supernatural soliciting / Cannot be ill; cannot be good" (p. 9). And certainly at this point he has done nothing wrong—he even points out that if Chance wants him king, he'll be king without moving a finger. But even that concession proves he's being tempted to take action into his own hands, to "stir." The other side of that problem, though, is *what if he is supposed to take action?* And the more emphasis you place on the supernatural sign of the witches' first prophecy, the more drastic an action you can consider—because it has already been justified by the cosmos. And perhaps Macbeth never would have committed murder if Lady Macbeth hadn't been quite so on board with the assassination. She also seems to put too much stock in the supernatural: "Come, you spirits / That tend on mortal thoughts, unsex me here; / And fill me, from the crown to the toe, topfull / Of direst cruelty!" (p. 14). First Glamis. Then Cawdor. Wouldn't—*shouldn't*—Scotland be theirs next?

What makes these issues foggier is the theme of doublespeak, when two meanings are present in a scene—one intended by the speaker, and one clear to the audience. And this theme, which insinuates itself into every nook and cranny of the play, is introduced by the witches. Who else? "Fair is foul, and foul is fair: / Hover through the fog and filthy air." Macbeth notices the same thing: "So foul and fair a day I have not seen." And the doublespeak of traitors is ever-present in the mind of Macbeth: "False face must hide what the false heart doth know." And Lady Macbeth knows her husband needs to "look like the innocent flower, / But be the serpent under [i]t."

The theme of doublespeak often creates cringe-worthy moments of dramatic irony, where the audience knows something vitally important that the speaker does not. The witches' prophecies are the obvious examples of this: We know Macbeth has already been given Cawdor—but Macbeth doesn't understand why he's addressed as Thane of Cawdor. And when Macbeth returns to the witches (talk about doubling down on your folly!), he gets three prophecies with double meanings. First, Macbeth himself makes sure Macduff becomes his worst enemy by murdering his family. Second, Macbeth doesn't think of caesarean section as a way to not be "born of woman." Third, Macbeth—the consummate soldier—doesn't think of camouflage as a way to get Birnam Wood to move. But in my opinion, no dramatic irony is as bad as King Duncan's. After the previous Thane of Cawdor's execution has been scheduled, he remarks, "No more that Thane of Cawdor shall deceive / Our bosom interest." And he goes on to choose Macbeth as a second Thane of Cawdor, speaking of the "care" of his "peerless kinsman." We can only watch in horror.

So, admittedly, the doublespeak complicates things. And remember, Macbeth is not one to contemplate a problem for long (almost the opposite of Hamlet in that regard!). Considering his soldiery predisposition to force, the witches really are the starting point in a journey that ends with his head getting chopped off and stuck on his own battlements. But his first steps are understandable if you trust the witches.

If you trust the witches... Something about that phrase shouldn't sit well with us. Is trusting witches usually a great option? Perhaps that's why Macbeth referred to them as "weird sisters" in his letter to his wife, instead of "witches." The connotation of "fate" is a bit better than that of "eye of newt, and toe of frog, / Wool of bat, and tongue of dog." But you'd think Macbeth would balance his political hunger with a little more wariness. Wouldn't a general at least consider a trap or ambush?

Partly due to his own mixed prophecy, I'm sure, Banquo has a much more negative view of the witchy news. "Oftentimes," he says, "to win us to our harm, / The instruments of darkness tell us truths; / Win us with honest trifles, to betray [u]s / In deepest consequence" (p. 9). And in fact that is what Macbeth gets into: deepest consequence, "in blood / Steeped so far that, should I wade no more, / Returning were as tedious as go o'er."

If there was ever any doubt, Banquo was right: the witches are out to ruin men's lives. First, Shakespeare characterizes the witches with the disturbingly whimsical Act I, Scene III (pp. 4-5) in which a housewife refuses a witch a chestnut, and the witch goes in guise of a tailless rat to gnaw a hole in her husband's ship in revenge. But all is made clear by Hecate (goddess of black magic from Greek mythology). In Act III, Scene V she berates the witches that they didn't ask her to join in on Macbeth's destruction, and then leaves to summon spirits which will completely ruin Macbeth. Whether or not the witches' first spell (p. 6) had a similar effect on Macbeth's decisions, we know after this point (p. 53) Macbeth will have no concern for his own life, and continue to think he can be king in the face of all reason. And immediately after this, we get confirmation of invincible storm clouds on the horizon: Malcolm has gotten help to overthrow the usurper from Edward, King of England, and his general Siward. We can only guess whether prophecy could have come true without Macbeth ruining his whole life, but we certainly know the witches enjoyed the way it all turned out. Rather pathetically, Macbeth comes to recognize this even as he's sending murderers after Banquo and Fleance: "For them [the witches] the gracious Duncan have I murther'd; /[…] Only for them."

However, even as we look at the factors that confused Macbeth in the moment, there really is no way around the fact that Macbeth was ultimately responsible. That, I suppose, is the human condition. Plus, even if the supernatural seemed to be in favor of Macbeth (in that the witches' first prophecy was fulfilled), the many more supernatural signs that come *after* the murder clearly show that the supernatural cries out over Duncan's blood: bloody daggers, terrible dreams, strange voices, prophesyings, augury, and of course Banquo's ghost all work together to disabuse any notion of the murder being morally neutral. Eventually,

Macbeth can't even pray: "I had most need of blessing, and 'Amen' / Stuck in my throat."

The slow revelation of Macbeth and Lady M.'s guilt gives this play a fascinating and horrible undercurrent, as they move from rejoicing to uncertainty to madness (in Lady Macbeth's case) and hopeless rashness (in Macbeth's). "Even-handed justice / Commends the ingredients of our poison'd chalice / To our own lips," Macbeth admits. *Blood will have blood.*

Perhaps Shakespeare had front-row seats to the political machinations of the English capital, and used his observations in his plays—because the emotions he pictures seem very real. *Macbeth* takes the political "predisposition" toward ambition and puts it on a spit, so we can turn it around and watch it blacken into murder and madness.

So, if Macbeth thought all life was meaningless sound and fury, he was wrong. But if he meant that his own efforts signified nothing, then we can agree with him. Malcolm's words apply to the second Thane of Cawdor as much as the first: "Nothing in his life / Became him like the leaving it."

However, once we view Macbeth through the lens of a fictional character, the grim beauty of the play signifies so much more than nothing.

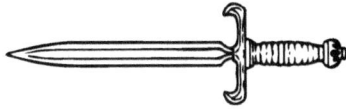

QUOTABLES

1. Come what come may,
   Time and the hour runs through the roughest day."
   > ~ Macbeth; Act I, Scene III (p. 10)

2. Nothing in his life
   Became him like the leaving it.
   > ~ Malcolm; Act I, Scene IV (p. 11)

3. Yet do I fear thy nature;
   It is too full o' the milk of human kindness
   To catch the nearest way: thou wouldst be great;
   Art not without ambition; but without
   The illness should attend it. What thou wouldst highly,
   That wouldst thou holily; wouldst not play false,
   And yet wouldst wrongly win.
   > ~ Lady Macbeth; Act I, Scene V (p. 13)

4. Will all great Neptune's ocean wash this blood
   Clean from my hand? No; this my hand will rather

The multitudinous seas incarnadine,
Making the green one red.

~ Macbeth; Act II, Scene I (p. 26)

5. There's daggers in men's smiles: the near in blood,
The nearer bloody.

~ Donalbain; Act II, Scene I (p. 33)

6. Double, double, toil and trouble;
Fire, burn; and cauldron, bubble.

~ the Three Witches; Act IV, Scene I (p. 56)

7. By the pricking of my thumbs,
Something wicked this way comes.

~ Second Witch; Act IV, Scene I (p. 58)

8. Out, damned spot! out, I say! […] Here's the smell
of the blood still: all the perfumes of Arabia will not
sweeten this little hand.

~ Lady Macbeth; Act V, Scene I (p. 78)

9. Life's but a walking shadow; a poor player,
That struts and frets his hour upon the stage,
And then is heard no more: it is a tale
Told by an idiot, full of sound and fury,
Signifying nothing.

~ Macbeth; Act V, Scene V (p. 86)

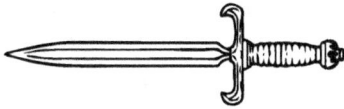

21 SIGNIFICANT QUESTIONS AND ANSWERS

1. Describe Macbeth's character. Which traits sum him up best?

   > Macbeth is first and foremost a soldier, from Scene 1 he is covered in blood (with bloody hands, just like the Israelite King David). Before he becomes a murdering "man of blood" (p. 51), this trait isn't bad. He's a fantastic general who leads by example. Of course, he's also very ambitious (by his own admission). Again, this is bad only when that ambition is completely selfish (Phil. 2:3). But these two traits mix together to create the murderous fool who is executed at the end of this play.

2. How does King Duncan's statement regarding the pre-Macbeth Thane of Cawdor ("He was a gentleman on whom I built an absolute trust") demonstrate dramatic irony?

King Duncan is regretting the betrayal of that
previous thane whom he had trusted, and rejoicing
in Macbeth, a thane whom he trusts and who will
betray him even more spectacularly. The audience
knows this and the characters don't (dramatic irony).

3.   Right before he sends men to Macduff's castle,
      Macbeth decides, "From this moment / The very
      firstlings of my heart shall be / The firstlings of my
      hand. And even now, / To crown my thoughts with
      acts, be it thought and done: / The castle of Macduff I
      will surprise… (Act IV, Scene I). How is this resolution
      "doubling down" on Macbeth's character problem?

"Thoughts versus acts" is a big theme in the play,
and Macbeth's predisposition is always towards
acts, of course. Early in the play he takes a bit of
persuading to murder Duncan, but by Act IV the
thought/act relationship is completely unbalanced.
For Macbeth, there is no difference between the
two any longer, and thus he creates his own mortal
enemy (and eventual killer) by murdering innocents
at the drop of a hat (Macduff's family). This and
guilt are his main character developments throughout the play.

4.   Do any other characters besides Macbeth prefer acts to
      thoughts?

Lady Macbeth—especially when she feels the guilt
("These deeds must not be thought / After these
ways; so, it will make us mad"). Malcolm wants

Macduff to act rather than just think about his
family's deaths (pp. 75-76).

5.   Compare and contrast Macbeth and Lady Macbeth.
     What's she like?

Lady Macbeth is more important to the play than
anyone else excluding Macbeth. She is the catalyst
that drives the play from event to event—without
her you feel that Macbeth would have been too
lazy (or too afraid or too loyal, depending on your
reading of his character) to act on the prophecies.
Bucknill describes her as "the terrible remorseless
impersonation of passionate ambition."[14] But other
readers have observed that her ambition seems to
be mostly for her husband's position, and not for
herself. And together they are successful—in the
(very) short run. Psychologically, she is both quicker
to flame and quicker to ash: She has decided
Duncan must die long before Macbeth agrees, but
Deighton notes that she doesn't participate in the
later murders. And in fact the blood of just one man
on her hands destroys her from the inside out.

6.   Do Macbeth's predispositions towards selfish ambition
     and action necessarily lead to murder?

Of course Macbeth had a choice (see next question). But the path from selfish ambition to murder
is not as far as we might like to pretend: They're

---

14. Quoted in K. Deighton, *Macbeth with an Introduction and Notes*
(London: Macmillan, 1893).

both fruit from the same tree. Look at the companionship selfish ambition keeps in Galatians 5:19-21: "Now the works of the flesh are evident, which are: adultery, fornication, uncleanness, lewdness, idolatry, sorcery, hatred, contentions, jealousies, outbursts of wrath, selfish ambitions, dissensions, heresies, envy, murders, drunkenness, revelries, and the like; of which I tell you beforehand, just as I also told you in time past, that those who practice such things will not inherit the kingdom of God." You could pretty much summarize the play with that list—envy? contentions? murders? selfish ambitions? sorcery, even? *Macbeth* to a T. The only thing missing is the various kinds of fornication.

7. Did the witches and Hecate compel Macbeth to murder Duncan, Banquo, and the others?

I'm sure some critics put heavy emphasis on the spells of the witches, but any sort of "he was forced to murder because of magic" explanation is a superficial reading. Macbeth clearly felt his own guilt and agency. However, the witches were a significant piece of the circumstances that led to Macbeth's temptation and fall. If you had to put words to what the witches actually did, you could say they deceived, misled, confused, and tempted him to his demise for their own sadistic enjoyment. Based on the text, I don't believe the witches had power to jinx him into murder (like some sort of voodoo puppet)—remember that with the chestnut-sailor's-wife incident. The witches weren't allowed to sink his ship outright: All they could do was gnaw a hole in the side and delay him, and see if those circumstances would lead to his demise.

8. What conflict occurs in *Macbeth*? List at least ten different conflicts.[15]

Conflict is all over the place in *Macbeth*. Character-to-character conflict is easy. The series of four conflicts with Macbeth versus Duncan, Malcolm, Banquo, and Macduff each have their own different motivations and details that affect the plot. Macbeth versus himself and Lady Macbeth versus herself provide two more instances for Shakespeare to work with the human psyche and with guilt. Macbeth versus Lady Macbeth (before the murder) and Macbeth versus Banquo's Ghost offer more opportunities to understand his character. King versus traitors is a broader conflict. So is witches versus humans. So is tyrant versus Scotland. And loyalty versus desire in Macbeth's mind. That's twelve of the biggest conflicts, without getting into the tiny ones (like internal strife between the witches and Hecate) or broader, less helpful ones (good versus evil).

---

15. Remember that the five elements of a story are Setting, Characters, Plot, Conflict, and Themes (well, depending on who is listing them... Perspective, Tone, and Irony can be just as important if not more). Understanding Shakespeare's development of each element is the key to appreciating the play as a whole.

9.   Compare and contrast Banquo and Macbeth. Is
     Banquo Macbeth's literary foil?[16]

> The similarities are too obvious to be coincidence.
> The two generals of Duncan's army are clearly com-
> rades, they both receive prophecies, they both have
> kingship in their future, except in opposite ways.
> Banquo functions as Macbeth's voice of reason and
> is then murdered by Macbeth. A black mark against
> Banquo is that he guessed at Macbeth's guilt and
> yet did nothing, willing to stand by and see if his
> "oracles" came true as well (p. 36). As a ghost he
> continues to be a foil for Macbeth, this time expos-
> ing Macbeth's unbalanced mind to his noblemen,
> which is a sign to us in the audience of Macbeth's
> unbalanced nature.

10. Trace the theme of blood in this book.

> The theme is that "blood will have blood" (p. 51).
> The futility of killing is that it begets killing. The
> prophecy associated with Banquo's son is contrast-
> ed with the barrenness of Macbeth's life: Macbeth
> doesn't have children. His legacy is blood—sound
> and fury only. But Macbeth is introduced to us after
> having "unseam'd" a man such that he had "bathe[d]
> in reeking wounds," and the man has visions of

---

16. In case you've forgotten, a literary foil is "someone or something
that makes another's good or bad qualities all the more noticeable."
In *Cambridge Academic Content Dictionary* (Cambridge: Cambridge
University Press, 2008), www.dictionary.cambridge.org/us/dictionary/
english/foil (accessed April 12, 2016).

"dudgeon gouts of blood" even before he has murdered anybody.

11. This play seems to view the supernatural as mostly prophetic signs and sorcery—but what about God Himself?

> The characters know there is a God above even though they aren't quoting Bible verses (or even remembering His rule over all in the midst of decisions to murder). The clearest indication of this (besides some references to "powers" being on their side) is the obvious line between right and wrong action engraved in each character's minds. As Macbeth pitifully admits, "I had most need of blessing, and 'Amen' / Stuck in my throat."

12. Does this play occur in a world ruled by the Trinity? And how important is that question?

> This is a very important question, but the way to answer it is not by asking, "Does a character tell Macbeth the sixth commandment and the Gospel before or after he kills Duncan?" Nor is the solution to ask whether the Christian God is mentioned. (J.R.R. Tolkien's *The Lord of the Rings* would fail that foolish test.) Instead, this question is about truthfulness: Is this play true? Does it represent the reality (or an aspect of the reality) of the world that God did create? Or, is it telling a lie? And, by the way, there are occasional references in *Macbeth* to God and to Jesus ("memorize another Golgotha")

that refer directly to the true God and hint at deeper themes, which we don't have space to discuss.

13. How does the theme of "being a man" show up in this play?

Macbeth and Lady Macbeth seem to have a view that man is all action: Lady Macbeth wishes she were a man (she wants Macbeth to be king so badly she says she would kill a child of her own), and gets Macbeth to murder Duncan by challenging his manliness. On the other hand, Macduff balances a "thinking" man with an "action" man. When Malcolm provokes him to "dispute it [the death of his family] like a man," Macduff replies, "I shall do so; / But I must also feel it as a man: / I cannot but remember such things were, / That were most precious to me." And of course, Macbeth doesn't want any knowledge of his own feelings: "To know my deed, 'twere best not know myself." But Macbeth does seem to see the wrongness of the all-brute-force type of manliness when he distastefully deals with the murderers (whom he is hiring). He says, "Ay, in the catalogue ye go for men" (p. 40), which is hardly a ringing endorsement… but at the same time, it should be noted that these men are exactly what Macbeth is. They're the logical extension of Macbeth's kind of man.

14. Was the witches' prophecy to Banquo (that he'll father kings, but won't be one) wrong? Why is Malcolm crowned at the end of the play instead of Fleance?

This prophecy is another great example of double-speak and dramatic irony—because King James I (Shakespeare's monarch) traced his family tree through Banquo. So King James is the final confirmation of the three witches' prophetic insight (in a flattering way, of course—he was Shakespeare's monarch, after all).

15. What's the significance of the random English doctor telling Malcolm and the others that King Edward is healing King's evil at that time (p. 71, Act IV, Scene III)?

King's evil is basically tuberculosis in your lymph nodes, and tradition has it that the touch of a king can cure it. Here it's used flatteringly as a sign of lawful kingship, partly because it's something King James I liked to do.

16. Can you identify themes or motifs Shakespeare may have borrowed from current events of his day? Remember that James I (VI of Scotland) had likely survived the Gunpowder Plot while this play was being written.

Loyalty is obviously the biggest theme. What delineates a king from a tyrant is another one that would have been on people's minds.

17. What's the significance of the Porter?

Shakespeare's tragedies almost always have comic relief in the midst of tragedy. The porter is pretty

jarring (there's some evidence that Shakespeare
or someone else completed *Macbeth*'s manuscript
using previously existing material), but he fills
that humorous purpose and suggests to us that
Macbeth is a type of Satan. He also dates the play
with Elizabethan pop-culture references to the very
low price of wheat in 1606 and to "an equivocator,"
a reference to a Jesuit priest who was hanged in
the aftermath of the Gunpowder plot. (The priest
defended lying as actually telling the truth because
God knew what you meant.)

18. In Holinshed's earlier historical account of Macbeth's
    betrayal, Banquo was complicit in King Duncan's
    murder—and the King wasn't murdered in Macbeth's
    castle, he was ambushed and killed elsewhere. What's
    the significance of those two changes?

    Banquo, as a distant ancestor of King James, ob-
    viously couldn't be a traitorous scumbag in 1606.
    And breaking the rules of hospitality (instead
    of an ambush) adds another layer to Macbeth's
    perfidy—along with echoing classical Greek and
    Roman themes.

19. Do you like this play? What is there to appreciate
    about it?

    Well, this isn't the sort of literature that evokes sat-
    isfaction and contentment, so it's easy to dismiss it
    superficially with "I don't like it." It helps to remem-
    ber that the Greek tragedies were trying to "cleanse"

their audiences using the emotions of fear and pity
felt towards a character like us (catharsis). With this
in mind, we can begin to see the power of *Macbeth*
(even if Shakespeare wasn't thinking in Aristotle's
categories). It is hard to fail to appreciate the play
for the old-fashioned sense of dread it evokes, its
relatable characters, and its enduring script.

20. Has *Macbeth* the play affected culture downstream
    from itself? Give specific examples.

The quotes from the "Quotables" section are often
referenced (along with other parts of the play).
Shakespeare coined "the milk of human kindness,"
of course, and William Faulkner's *The Sound and
the Fury*, Ray Bradbury's *Something Wicked This
Way Comes*, and Agatha Christie's *By the Pricking
of My Thumbs* are all taken from the play. In "The
Beauty and the Beast," Gastogne quotes Lady
Macbeth during a song, and Harry Potter #3 uses
"double double toil and trouble" to great effect as
its theme chorus (composed by John Williams).
There's a lot more, of course. If you do a web
search for "acne out damned spot," you'll find
every skin-cream marketing team on the Internet
had the same genius idea. According to IMDB,
from before World War I till now there have been
well over thirty movie adaptations of the play
(with new versions in production). I'll conclude
by pointing out that Season 20, Episode 20 of The
Simpsons features Homer (the deadbeat dad) as
a reluctant Macbeth in the town play, forced by

Marge (his wife) to murder any co-actor who gets
a better critical reception than he does.

21. What's the significance of Macbeth's name?

Macbeth means "son of life." This is perhaps the
best example of doublespeak in the play. There
are no people less associated with life than the
Macbeths. Whatever they touch, dies. This includes
themselves—Macbeth created his own nemesis
and Lady Macbeth committed suicide. The name
"Macbeth" is perhaps the best and shortest summa-
ry of the play's power. *Macbeth* is the hair-raising
story of a man and a woman—who should have
been life-givers—turning into death-dealers by
their own choice and finding they lost everything
that mattered in the process.

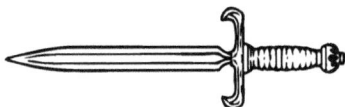

FURTHER DISCUSSION
AND REVIEW

Master what you have read by reviewing and integrating the different elements of this classic.

SETTING AND CHARACTERS

Be able to compare and contrast the personalities (including strengths, weaknesses, and mannerisms) of each character. How does the setting affect the characters?

PLOT

Be able to describe the beginning, middle, and end of the book along with specific details that move the plot forward and make it compelling. This includes the success or downfall (or both) of each character.

CONFLICT

Go through the character list and describe the tension between any and all main characters. Then, think about whether any characters have internal conflict (in their own minds). Is there any overt conflict (fighting), or conflict with impersonal forces?

THEME STATEMENTS

Be able to describe what this classic is telling us about the world. Is the message true? What truth can we take from the plot, characters, conflict, and themes (even if the author didn't believe that truth)? Do any objects take on added meaning because of repetition or their place in the story (i.e., do any objects become symbols)? How does the author use perspective, tone, and irony to tell the truth?

Be able to interact with and give examples for the following theme statements:

> A leader must balance doing and thinking; an over-reliance on action makes you susceptible to misinterpretation and deceit, and is ultimately a form of insanity.

> Unfulfilled and unrestrained ambition to rule leads to treason; but since a leader and his followers are bound together by loyalty, spilled blood destroys not only the one betrayed, but also the community as a whole, and eventually the betrayer as well through revenge.

> Despite free will, humans are unable to use prophecies for their own advantage; similarly, manipulative interaction with the supernatural world is fraught with ambiguity and dramatic and verbal irony.

Finally, compose your own theme statement about some element, large or small, of this classic. Then, use the Bible and common sense to assess the truth of that theme statement. Identify your own key words or borrow from the following list as a starting point: *humans and the supernatural; double meaning and ambiguity; doers and thinkers; ambition and loyalty; betrayal and death; prophecy and choice; kingship and heirs; murder and revenge; insanity; blood.*

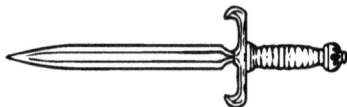

A NOTE FROM THE PUBLISHER:
TAKING THE CLASSICS QUIZ

Once you have finished the worldview guide, you can prepare for the end-of-book test. Each test will consist of a short-answer section on the book itself and the author, a short-answer section on plot and the narrative, and a long-answer essay section on worldview, conflict, and themes.

Each quiz, along with other helps, can be downloaded for free at www.canonpress.com/ClassicsQuizzes. If you have any questions about the quiz or its answers or the Worldview Guides in general, you can contact Canon Press at service@canonpress.com or 208.892.8074.

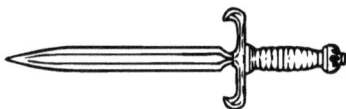

ABOUT THE AUTHOR

Brian Kohl is the editorial director for Canon Press. Over the past seven years he has also taught Latin, History, and Rhetoric to students at Logos School, Logos Online School, and New Saint Andrews College. He and his wife Christy have two sons. A little of his poetry has been published by *The Curator*.